THE 4 CHORD SONGBOOK

The Beatles • Johnny Cash • ...on & Garfunkel

Hank Williams • John Denver • Harry Belafonte

Dave Matthews Band • Little Feat • Buffalo Springfield

> |G |C
> All my bags are packed, I'm ready to go,
>
> |G |C
> I'm standing here out-side your door,

Peter, Paul, and Mary • Harry Belafonte

Tony Orlando and Dawn • Bob Dylan • The Youngbloods

Creedence Clearwater Revival • Janis Joplin • Hanson

The Who • Tom Paxton • Bobbie Gentry • The Byrds

Crosby, Stills & Nash • Woody Guthrie • Bob Marley

Cherry Lane Music Company
Director of Publications/Project Editor: Mark Phillips
Project Coordinator: Rebecca Skidmore

ISBN 978-1-60378-251-7

Visit our website at www.cherrylaneprint.com

CONTENTS

Act Naturally

Words and Music by
Vonie Morrison and Johnny Russell

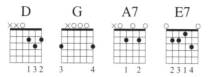

Verse 1

D | | G | | |
They're gonna put me in the movies;

D | | A7 | |
They're gonna make a big star out of me.

| D | | | G | |
We'll make a scene about a man that's sad and lonely,

| A7 | | | D | |
And all I gotta do is   act natural - ly.

Verse 2

|| D | | G | |
We'll make a score about a man that's sad and lonely

| D | | A7 | |
And beggin' down up - on his bended knee.

| D | | G | |
I'll play the part but I won't need re - hearsin',

| A7 | | | D | |
'Cause all I have to do is   act natural - ly.

Bridge

```
  ||A7            |          |D         |
Well, I bet you I'm gonna be a big star.

   |A7           |                |D       |
Might win an Ocsar; you can't never tell.

   |A7           |          |D       |
The movies are gonna make me a big star,

   |E7       |          |A7       |
'Cause I can play the part so well.
```

Verse 3

```
   ||D              |          |G      |          |
Well, I hope you come and see me in the movies,

D             |          |A7       |
Then I know that you will plainly see

  |D           |      |G       |
The biggest fool that ever hit the big time,

   |A7         |          |D       |        ||
And all I gotta do is    act natural - ly.
```

Away in a Manger

Words by John T. McFarland (v.3)
Music by James R. Murray

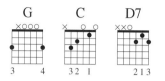

Verse 1

|G | |C |G
A - way in a manger, no crib for a bed,

|D7 | |G |
The little Lord Jesus laid down His sweet head.

| | |C |G
The stars in the sky looked down where He lay,

|D7 |G |C D7 |G
The little Lord Jesus, a - sleep on the hay.

Verse 2

‖G | |C |G
The cattle are lowing, the Baby a - wakes,

|D7 | |G |
But little Lord Jesus no crying He makes.

| | |C |G
I love Thee, Lord Jesus, look down from the sky,

|D7 |G |C D7 |G
And stay by my cradle till morning is nigh.

Verse 3

‖G | |C |G
Be near me, Lord Jesus, I ask Thee to stay

|D7 | |G |
Close by me for-ever and love me, I pray.

| | |C |G
Bless all the dear children in Thy tender care,

|D7 |G |C D7 |G ‖
And fit us for heaven to live with Thee there.

A Boy Named Sue

Words and Music by
Shel Silverstein

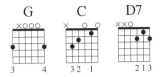

Verse 1

|G |
Well, my "daddy" left home when I was three,

|C |
And he didn't leave much to Ma and me,

|D7 | |G |
Just this old guitar and an empty bottle of booze.

|G |
Now, I don't blame him because he run and hid,

|C | |D7 |
But the meanest thing that he ever did was be-fore he left,

|D7 |G |
He went and named me Sue.

Verse 2

||G |
Well, he must have thought it was quite a joke,

|C |
And it got lots of laughs from a lot of folks.

|D7 | |G |
It seems I had to fight my whole life through.

|G |
Some gal would giggle and I'd get red.

|C |
And some guy would laugh and I'd bust his head,

|D7 | |G |
I tell you, life ain't easy for a boy named Sue.

Verse 3

||G |

Well, I grew up quick and I grew up mean.

|C | |

My fist got hard and my wits got keen.

D7 | |G |

Roamed from town to town to hide my shame.

|G | |

But I made me a vow to the moon and stars,

C |

I'd search the honky - tonks and bars

|D7 | |G |

And kill that man that give me that awful name.

Verse 4

||G |

But it was Gatlinburg in mid July,

|C | |

And I had just hit town and my throat was dry.

D7 | |G |

I'd thought I'd stop and have myself a brew.

|G | |

At an old saloon on a street of mud,

C | |

There at a table dealing stud

D7 | |G |

Sat the dirty, mangy dog that named me Sue.

Verse 5

||G
Well, I knew that snake was my own sweet dad

|C
From a worn-out picture that my mother had.

|D7 |G
And I knew that scar on his cheek and his evil eye.

|G
He was big and bent and gray and old

|C
And I looked at him and my blood ran cold,

|D7 |G
And I said "My name is Sue.   How do you do?

|G
Now you're gonna die."   Yeah that's what I told him.

Verse 6

||G
Well, I hit him hard right be - tween the eyes and

C
He went down, But to my surprise

D7 |G
He come up with a knife and cut off a piece of my ear.

|G
But I busted a chair right a - cross his teeth,

|C
And we crashed through the wall and into the street,

D7 |G
Kicking and a-gouging in the mud and the blood and the beer.

Verse 7

||G | |
I tell you I've fought tougher men but I

C |
Really can't remember when.

 |**D7** | |**G** |
He kicked like a mule and he bit like a croco - dile.

 |**G** |
I heard him laugh and then I heard him cuss,

 |**C** |
And he went for his gun and I pulled mine first.

 |**D7** | |**G** |
He stood there looking at me   and I saw him smile.

Verse 8

||**G** | | |
And he said, "Son,   this world is rough and if a man's gonna make it,

 |**G** | |**D7** |**G** |
He's gotta be tough, and I know I wouldn't be there to help you a - long.

 |**G** |
So I give you that name and I said goodbye,

|**C** |
I knew you'd have to get tough   or die.

 |**D7** | |**G** |
And it's that name that helped to make you strong. "

Verse 9

||**G** | |
Yeah,   he said, "Now, you just fought one helluva fight,

 |**C** |
And I know you hate me and you've got the right

 |**D7** | |**G** |
To kill me now and I wouldn't blame you if you do.

 |**G** |
But you ought to thank me be - fore I die

 |**C** |
For the gravel in your guts and the spit in your eye

 |**D7** | |**G** |
'Cause I'm the —— that named you Sue."

 |**G** | |**C**
Yeah, what could I do?   What could I do?

Verse 10

        ||**C** |**D7**
I got all choked up and I threw down my gun

    |**D7** |**G**
And called him my pa and he called me his son,

G | | |**D7**
And I come away with a different point of view.

     |**G** |
And I think about him now and then.

      |**C** | |**D7 N.C.**
Every time I tried, every time I win,   and if I ever have a son

N.C. |**G** ||
I think I'm gonna name him ... Bill or George! ... anything but Sue!

Catch the Wind

Words and Music by Donovan Leitch

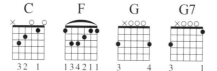

Verse 1

|C | |F |
In the chilly hours and minutes,

|C | |F | |
Of un - certainty, I want to be

C | |F |G |C | |G7 |
In the warm hold of your loving mind.

|C | |F |
To feel you all a - round me,

|C |F | |
And to take your hand a - long the sand,

C | |F |G |C | |G7 |
Ah, but I may as well try and catch the wind.

Verse 2

‖**C** | |**F** |
When sundown   pales the sky,

|**C** | |**F** | |
I want to hide a - while, behind your smile.

C | |**F** |**G** |**C** | |**G7** |
And everywhere I'd look, your eyes I'd find.

|**C** | |**F** |
For me to   love you now,

|**C** |**F** | |
Would be the sweetest thing, 'twould make me sing,

C | |**F** |**G** |**C** | |**G7** |
Ah, but I may as well try and catch the wind.

Verse 3

‖**C** | |**F** | |
When rain has   hung the leaves with tears,

C | |**F** | |
I want you near to kill my fears,

C | |**F** |**G** |**C** | |**G7** |
To help me   to leave all my blues be - hind.

|**C** | |**F** |
For standing   in your heart

|**C** | |**F** | |
Is where I want to be, and long to be,

C | |**F** |**G** |**C** | ‖
Ah, but I may as well try and catch the wind.

Cecilia

Words and Music by Paul Simon

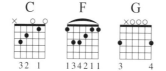

Chorus 1

C |F   C
Celia, you're breaking my heart.

       |F   C |G
You're shaking my con - fidence dai - ly.

        |F C |F   C
Oh Ce - cil - ia, I'm down on my knees.

       |F   C |G   ‖
I'm begging you please   to come home.

Chorus 2

C |F   C
Celia, you're breaking my heart.

       |F   C |G
You're shaking my con - fidence dai - ly.

        |F C |F   C
Oh Ce - cil - ia, I'm down on my knees.

       |F   C |G |C   ‖
I'm begging you please   to come home,   come on home.

Verse

C |F |C
Making love in the af - ternoon   with Cecil - ia

F |G   C |
Up in my   bedroom (making love).

C |F
I got up to wash   my face.

           |C |G   C ||
When I come back to bed someone's tak - en my place.

Chorus 3

C |F   C
Celia, you're breaking my heart.

     |F   C |G
You're shaking my con - fidence dai - ly.

     |F   C |F   C
Oh Ce - cil - ia, I'm down on my knees.

     |F   C |G |C
I'm begging you please to come home,   come on home.

Interlude

     ||F | |G
Poh poh poh poh poh poh poh poh poh poh poh poh poh.

Bridge

     ||F   C |F   C
Jubi - la - tion, she loves me again.

    |F   C |G
I fall on the floor   and I'm laugh - ing.

    |F   C |F   C
Jubi - la - tion, she loves me again.

    |F   C |G
I fall on the floor   and I'm laugh - ing.

Tag

     ||F   C |F   C
Oh oh oh   oh oh oh oh oh oh

    |F   C |G |C ||
Oh oh oh oh oh oh oh oh oh,   come on home.

Cold, Cold Heart

Words and Music by
Hank Williams

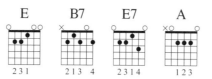

Verse 1

|E | | |B7
I tried so hard, my dear, to show that you're my every dream.

|B7 | | |E
Yet you're afraid each thing I do is just some evil scheme.

|E | |E7 |A
A memory from your lonesome past keeps us so far a - part.

|B7 | | |E
Why can't I free your doubtful mind and melt your cold, cold heart?

Verse 2

‖E | | |B7
An - other love be - fore my time made your heart sad and blue.

|B7 | | |E
And so my heart is paying now for things I didn't do.

|E | |E7 |A
In anger unkind words are said that make the teardrops start.

|B7 | | |E
Why can't I free your doubtful mind and melt your cold, cold heart?

Verse 3

‖E | | |B7
You'll never know how much it hurts to see you sit and cry.

|B7 | | |E
You know you need and want my love, yet you're afraid to try.

|E | |E7 |A
Why do you run and hide from life? To try it just ain't smart.

|B7 | | |E
Why can't I free your doubtful mind and melt your cold, cold heart?

Verse 4

||**E** | | |**B7**
There was a time when I believed that you belonged to me.

|**B7** | | |**E**
But now I know your heart is shackled to a memo - ry.

|**E** | |**E7** |**A**
The more I learn to care for you the more we drift a - part.

|**B7** | | |**E** ||
Why can't I free your doubtful mind and melt your cold, cold heart.

Dancing with the Mountains

Words and Music by
John Denver

D   G   G6

Verse 1

D | |
Everybody's got the dancin' fever,

D | |
Everybody loves to rock and roll.

D | |
Play it louder, baby, play it faster,

D | ||
Funky music's gotta stretch your soul.

Verse 2

D | |
Just relax and let the rhythm take you,

D | |
Don't you be afraid to lose control.

D | |
If your heart has found some empty spaces,

D | ||
Dancin's just a thing to make you whole.

Chorus 1

G | **D** | |
I am one who dances with the moun-tains.

G | **D** | |
I am one who dances in the wind.

G | **D** |
I am one who dances on the o-cean.

|**G** |**G6** |**D** | ||
My partner's more than pieces, more than friends.

Verse 3

D | |
Were you there the night they lost the lightning?

D | |
Were you there the day the earth stood still?

D | |
Did you see the famous and the fighting?

D | ||
Did you hear the prophet tell his tale?

Chorus 2

G | **D** | |
We are one when dancing with the moun-tains.

G | **D** | |
We are one when singing in the wind.

G | **D** |
We are one when thinking of each oth-er,

|**G** |**G6** |**D** | ||
More than partners, more than pieces, more than friends.

Day-O
(The Banana Boat Song)

Words and Music by
Irving Burgie and William Attaway

Intro

N.C.(D)
Day-o,　day-o.

Daylight come and me wan' go home.

Day, me say day, me say day, me say day, me say day, me say day-o.

Daylight come and me wan' go home.

Verse 1

D
Work all night on a drink of rum.

D　　　　　　　**A7**　**D**
Daylight come and me wan' go home.

D
Stack banana till de morning come.

D　　　　　　　**A7**　**D**
Daylight come and me wan' go home.

Verse 2

D　　　　　　　**A7**
Come, mister tally man, tally me banana.

D　　　　　　　**A7**　**D**
Daylight come and me wan' go home.

D　　　　　　　**A7**
Come, mister tally man, tally me banana.

D　　　　　　　**A7**　**D**
Daylight come and me wan' go home.

Verse 3

‖ **D** | |
Lift six-hand, seven-hand, eight-hand bunch.

D | **A7**   **D** |
Daylight come and me wan' go home.

D | |
Six-hand, seven-hand, eight-hand bunch.

D | **A7**   **D** ‖
Daylight come and me wan' go home.

Chorus

D | |
Day, me say day-o.

D | **A7**   **D** |
Daylight come and me wan' go home.

D | |
Day, me say day, me say day, me say…

D | **A7**   **D**
Daylight come and me wan' go home.

Verse 4

‖ **D** | |
A beautiful bunch of ripe banana.

D | **A7**   **D** |
Daylight come and me wan' go home.

D | |
Hide the deadly black tarantula.

D | **A7**   **D** ‖
Daylight come and me wan' go home.

Repeat Chorus

Repeat Verse 2

Outro

N.C.(D) | |
Day-o,   day-o.

D | **A7**   **D** |
Daylight come and me wan' go home.

N.C.(D) | | |
Day,   me say day, me say day, me say day, me say day, me say day-o.

D | **A7**   **D** ‖
Daylight come and me wan' go home.

Digging a Ditch

Lyrics by David J. Matthews
Music by Dave Matthews Band

G   C   Dadd4

Verse 1

G   **|C**
Run to your dreaming when   you're alone.
G   **|C**
Unplug the TV and turn off your phone.
G   **|C**
Get heavy on with digging your ditch.

Chorus 1

           ‖G   **|C**
'Cause I'm   digging a ditch where madness   gives a bit.
G   **|C**
Digging a ditch where silence   lives.
G   **|C**
Digging a ditch for when I'm   old.
G   **|C**
Digging this ditch, my story's   told.
           |G   **|C**   **‖**
Where all   these troubles that weigh down on me will rise.

Verse 2

       G   **|C**
    Run to your dreaming when you're alone.
         |G   **|C**
Where all these questions spinning a - round my head
        |Dadd4   **|C**
Will die,
        |Dadd4   **|C**   **||**
Will die,   will die.

Repeat Verse 1

Chorus 2

               ‖G   **|C**   **|**
'Cause I'm digging a ditch where madness gives a bit.
G   **|C**   **|**
   Digging a ditch where silence lives.
G   **|C**   **|**
   Digging a ditch for when I'm through.
G   **|C**
   Digging this ditch, I'm digging for you.
         |G   **|C**
Where all these worries that wear down on me
         |G   **|C**
Will rise.
         |G   **|C**   **||**
Where all these habits that pull heavy at my heart will die.

Verse 3

```
    G                             |C                    |
    Run  to  your  dreaming  when  you're  alone.
    G                                  |C
    Not  what  you  should  be  or  what    you've  become.
       |G              |C
Just    get  heavy  on  with  digging  your  ditch.
```

Chorus 3

```
                        ‖G                             |C                    |
   'Cause  I'm    digging  a  ditch  where  madness    gives  a  bit.
    G                              |C               |
    Digging  a  ditch  where  silence    lives.
          |G                           |C
Where  all    these  disappointments  that  grow  angry  out  of  me
            |Dadd4             |C
Will  rise,
            |Dadd4                  |C
Will  die,
            |Dadd4             |C                    ‖
Will  die,                          will  die.
```

Repeat Verse 1

Dixie Chicken

Words and Music by Lowell George
and Martin Kibbee

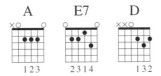

Verse 1

|A |
I've seen the bright lights of Mem - phis

|A |E7
And the Commodore Hotel,

|E7 |
And underneath a street   lamp

|E7 |A
I met   a Southern belle.

|D |A |
Oh, she took me to the riv - er,

A |E7
Where she cast her spell,

|E7 |
And in the Southern moon - light

|E7 |A
She sang   her song so well.

Chorus

‖**A** |
If you be my Dixie chick - en

|**A** |**E7**
I'll be your Tennessee lamb,

|**E7** |
And we can walk togeth - er

|**A** | | |
Down in Dixieland,　　　down in Dix - ieland.

Verse 2

‖**A** |
Well,　we made all the hot　spots;

|**A** |**E7**
My　money flowed like wine.

|**E7** |
And that low-down Southern whis - key

|**E7** |**A**
Began　to fog my mind.

|**D** |**A**
And I don't remember church　bells

|**A** |**E7**
Or the money I put down

|**E7** |
On the white picket fence and board - walk

|**E7** |**A**
Of the house at the edge of town.

|**D** |**A**
Oh, but boy, do I remem - ber

|**A** |**E7**
The strain of her refrain

|**E7** |
And the nights　we spent togeth - er

|**E7** |**A**
And the way she called my name.

Repeat Chorus

Verse 3

|A|
Well, been a year since she ran away;

|A| |E7|
Guess that guitar player sure could play.

|E7|
She always liked to sing along;

|E7| |A|
She's al - ways handy with a song.

D |A|
Then one night in the lobby

|A| |E7|
Of the Commodore Hotel,

|E7|
I chanced to meet a bartend - er

|E7| |A|
Who said he knew her well.

|D| |A|
And as he handed me a drink,

|A| |E7|
He be - gan to hum a song,

|E7|
And all the boys there at the bar

|E7| |A|
Be - gan to sing along.

Repeat Chorus

For What It's Worth

Words and Music by
Stephen Stills

E   A   D

Verse 1

E |A
    There's something happening here.
  |E |A
What it is ain't exactly clear.
    |E |A
There's a man with a gun over there
   |E |A
Telling me I got to beware.
        |E   D |
I think it's time we stop, children. What's that sound?
A |
Everybody look what's goin' down.
E |A |E |A ||

Verse 2

E |A
    There's battle lines being drawn.
  |E |A
Nobody's right if everybody's wrong.
E |A
    Young people speakin' their minds,
  |E |A
Getting so much resistance from behind.
        |E   D |
I think it's time we stop, hey. What's that sound?
A |
Everybody look what's goin' down.
E |A |E |A ||

Verse 3

```
        E                         |A
          What a field day for the heat.
       |E                    |A
A thousand people in the street
         |E                     |A
Singin' songs and carryin' signs,
         |E                     |A
Mostly say, "Hooray for our side."
                     |E        D              |
It's time we stop, hey. What's that sound?
A                           |
Everybody look what's goin' down.
E              |A              E              |A              ||
```

Verse 4

```
        E              |A                    |
Paranoia strikes deep,
        E              |A
Into your life it will creep.
         |E                        |A
It starts when you're always afraid.
                 |E
Step out of line, the man come
      |A
And take you away.
```

Outro

       ‖E   D |
We better stop, hey. What's that sound?
A
Everybody look what's goin'...
       |E   D |
You better stop, hey. What's that sound?
A
Everybody look what's goin'...
       |E   D |
You better stop, now. What's that sound?
A
Everybody look what's goin'...
       |E   D |
You better stop, children. What's that sound?
A |E   D |A |E   ‖
Everybody look what's goin'...

The Horizon Has Been Defeated

Words and Music by Jack Johnson

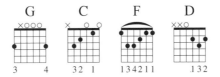

Verse 1

      |G   C
(The) ho - rizon has been defeat - ed

     |F   G |
By the pirates of the new age.

G   C
Alien casi - nos,

     |F   G
Well, maybe it's just time to say

     |G   C
That things can go bad

     |F   G
And make you want to run away.

     |G |C
But as we grow old - er,

     |F |D | ||
The trouble just seems to   stay.

Verse 2

G   C
Future complica - tions

  |F   G
In the strings between the cans.

  |G   C
But no prints can come from fin - gers

   |F   G
If ma - chines become our hands.

    |G   C
And then our feet become the wheels,

    |F   G
And then the wheels become the cars.

    |G   C
And then the rigs begin to drill

   |F |D | ||
Until the drilling goes too far.

G   C
Chorus Things can go bad

  |F   G
And make you want to run away.

  |G   C
But as we grow old - er,

    |F |D C |G |D C |G ||
(The) ho - rizon begins to fade, fade, fade, fade away.

Verse 3

```
     G                      C           |
Thingamajigsaw  puz - zled;

F                              G         |
Anger,  don't  you  step  too  close.

       |G
'Cause  people  are  lonely

          C        |F              G        |
And  on - ly  ani - mals  with  fancy  shoes.

G                      C           |
Hallelujah  zig  zag  noth - ing;

F                      G
Misery,  it's  on  the  loose.

       |G
'Cause  people  are  lonely

          C        |F                    |
And  on - ly  ani - mals  with  too  many  tools

D                                             |
   That  can  build  all  the  junk  that  we  sell.

D                                               ||
Oh,  sometime,  man,  make  you  want  to  yell,  and….
```

Chorus

```
G                      C
Things  can  go  bad

   |F                          G
And  make  you  want  to  run  away.

    |G              C
But  as  we  grow  old - er,

           |F              |D    C  |G        |D    C    |G          |
(The)  ho - rizon  begins  to   fade   away,           fade   away.

D      C    |G          |
  Fade,  fade,  fade.

D      C    |G          ||
  Fade,  fade,  fade.
```

The Gambler

Words and Music by
Don Schlitz

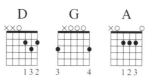

Verse 1

|**D** | |**G** |**D**
On a warm summer's eve - nin' on a train bound for no - where,

|**D** | | |**A**
I met up with the gam - bler; we were both too tired to sleep.

|**D** | |**G** |**D**
So we took turns star - in' out the window at the dark - ness

|**G** |**D** |**A** |**D**
Till boredom overtook us   and he began to speak.

Verse 2

||**D** | |**G** |**D**
He said, "Son I've made a life   out of readin' people's fac - es

|**D** | | |**A**
And knowin' what their cards   were   by the way they held their eyes.

|**D** | |**G** |**D**
And if you don't mind my say - in', I can see you're out   of ac - es.

|**G** |**D** |**A** |**D** |
For a taste of your whis - key   I'll give you some advice."

Verse 3

||**D** | |**G** |**D** |
So I handed him my bot - tle and he drank down my last swallow.

D | | |**A**
Then he bummed a cig - arette and asked me for a light.

|**D** | |**G** |**D**
And the night got deathly qui - et, and his face lost all expres - sion.

|**G** |**D** |**A** |**D**
Said, "If you're gonna play the game,   boy, ya gotta learn to play it right.

Chorus

            ‖**D** | |
You got to know when to hold 'em,

G |**D** |
Know when to fold 'em,

G |**D** | |**A**
Know when to walk away   and know when to run.

         |**D** | |**G** |**D**
You never count your money when you're sittin' at the ta - ble.

        |**D**   **G** |**D** |
There'll be time e - nough for count - in'

A |**D** | ‖
When the dealin's done.

Verse 4

D | |**G** |**D**
  Ev'ry gambler knows   that the secret to surviv - in'

|**D** | | |**A**
Is knowing what to throw away and knowin' what to keep,

  |**D** | |**G** |**D**
'Cause ev'ry hand's a win - ner and ev'ry hand's a los - er,

    |**G** |**D** |**A** |**D**
And the best that you can hope for is to die in your sleep."

Verse 5

      ‖**D** | |**G** |**D** |
And when he'd finished speakin', he turned back towards the win - dow,

D | | |**A**
  Crushed out his cigarette and faded off to sleep.

  |**D** | |**G** |**D**
And somewhere in the dark - ness the gambler, he broke even.

  |**G** |**D** |**A** |**D**
But in his final words I found an ace that I could keep.

Repeat Chorus

Garden Song

Words and Music by
Dave Mallett

D   G   A

Verse 1

D |G   D |G   A |D |
Inch by inch, row by row,   gonna make this garden grow,

G   A |D |G |A |
All it takes is a rake and a hoe and a piece of fertile ground.

D |G   D |G   A |D |
Inch by inch, row by row,   someone bless the seeds I sow,

G   A |D |G   A |D |G D | |A D ||
Someone warm them from below 'til the rain comes tumbling down.

Verse 2

D |G   D |G   A |D |
Pulling weeds and pickin' stones, man is made of dreams and bones,

G   A |D |G |A |
Feel the need to grow my own 'cause the time is close at hand.

D |G   D |G   A |D |
Grain for grain, sun and rain, find my way in nature's chain,

G   A |D |G   A |D |A |D ||
To my body and my brain to the music from the land.

Verse 3

```
         D              |G            D |G        A     |D          |
         Plant your rows straight and long,  thicker than   with prayer and song,

         G        A       |D                      |G             |A     |
         Mother Earth will make you strong if you give her love and care.

         D                |G      D |G          A   |D          |
         Old crow watchin' hungrily  from his perch  in yonder tree,

         G       A   |D               |G       A     |D  |A  |D  |A   ||
         In my garden I'm as free as that feathered beak up there.
```

Verse 4

```
         D            |G          D |G      A      |D          |
         Inch by inch, row by row,    gonna make this garden grow,

         G      A      |D                   |G                 |A    |
         All it takes is a rake and a hoe and a piece of fertile ground.

         D          |G         D |G       A    |D         |
         Inch by inch, row by row,    someone bless the seeds I sow,

         G          A   |D              |G       A      |D   |    |A D ||
         Someone warm   them from below 'til the rain comes tumbling down.
```

Guantanamera
Cuban Folksong

Em7   A7   D   G

Chorus

Em7   **|A7**   **|**
Guantanamera!   Guajira!

D   **G** **|A7**   **|**
Guantana - mera!

D   **G** **|A7**   **|**
Guantana - me - ra! Guajira!

D   **G** **|A7**
Guantana - me - ra!

Verse 1

‖G   **|A7**
Yo soy un hombre sincero

|D   **G** **|A7**
De donde crece la palma.

|G   **|A7**
Yo soy un hombre sincero

|G   **|A7**
De donde crece la palma.

|D   **G** **|A7**
Y antes de morirme quie - ro

|D   **G** **|A7** **‖**
Echar mis versos del al - ma.

Repeat Chorus

Verse 2

```
              ‖G            |A7
Mi  verso  es  de  un  verde  claro

                  |D          G      |A7
Y  de  un  car - min  encen - dido.

                  |G            |A7
Mi  verso  es  de  un  verde  claro

                  |G          |A7
Y  de  un  car - min  encen - dido.

              |D        G    |A7
Mi  verso  es  un  cierro  heri - do

                  |D            G    |A7 ‖
Que  busca  en  el  monte  am - pa - ro.
```

Repeat Chorus

Verse 3

```
              ‖G              |A7
Con  los  po - bres  de  la  tierra

                  |D            G    |A7
Quiero  yo  mi  suerte  e - char.

                  |G              |A7
Con  los  po - bres  de  la  tierra

                  |G          |A7
Quiero  yo  mi  suerte  e - char

              |D          G  |A7
El  arro - yo  de  la  si - er - ra

                  |D            G  |A7    ‖
Me  compla - ce  mas  que  el  mar.
```

Repeat Chorus

Heard It in a Love Song

Words and Music by Toy Caldwell

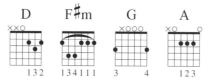

Verse 1

|D | | |
I ain't never been with a woman long enough

F#m | |
For my boots to get old.

G |
We've been togeth - er so long now,

|D | |
They both need re - soled.

D | |
If I ever settle down,

F#m |
You'd be my kind,

|G
And it's a good time for me

|A |D |
To head on down the line.

Chorus

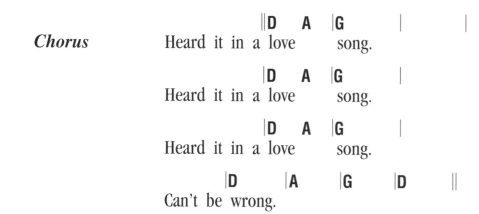

‖D A |G | |
Heard it in a love song.

|D A |G |
Heard it in a love song.

|D A |G |
Heard it in a love song.

|D |A |G |D ‖
Can't be wrong.

Verse 2

D
   I'm the kind of man

F♯m
    Who likes to get away,

G
    Likes to start dreaming about

 |D
To - morrow to - day.

D
   Never said that I loved you

 |F♯m
Even though it's so.

    |G |A
There's that duffle bag of mine;

     |D
It's time to go.

Repeat Chorus

Verse 3

D
   I'm gonna be leaving

F♯m
    At the break of dawn.

G
   Wish you could come,

      |D
But I don't need no woman taggin' a - long.

D
   Always something greener

   |F♯m
On the other side of that hill.

     |G
I was born a wrangler and a rounder

  |A |D
And I guess I always will.

Repeat Chorus

The Holly and the Ivy

18th Century English Carol

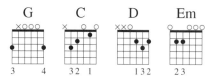

Verse 1

|G   C |G
The holly and the ivy

     |G   C |D
When they are both full grown,

    |G |C   G
Of all the trees that are in the wood,

Em |C   D |G   C
The holly bears the crown.

Chorus

‖G   C |G
The rising of the sun

    |G   C |D
And the running of the deer,

  |G |C   G Em
The playing of the merry or-gan,

   |C   D |G
Sweet singing in the choir.

Verse 2

‖G   C|G
The holly bears a blossom

 |G   C |D
As white as lil-y flow'r,

  |G |C   G
And Mary bore sweet Jesus Christ

Em |C   D |G   C
To be our sweet Sav-iour.

Repeat Chorus

Verse 3
    ‖G   C |G
The holly bears a berry

    |G   C |D
As red as an-y blood,

     |G |C   G
And Mary bore sweet Jesus Christ

Em|C   D |G   C
To do poor sin-ners good.

Repeat Chorus

Verse 4
    ‖G   C|G
The holly bears a prickle

    |G   C |D
As sharp as an-y thorn,

    |G |C   G
And Mary bore sweet Jesus Christ

Em |C   D |G   C
On Christmas Day in the morn.

Repeat Chorus

I Saw Three Ships

18th Century English Carol

Verse 1

|G   D7 |G   D7
I saw three ships come sailing in,

|G |D7
On Christmas Day, on Christmas Day.

|Em   D7 |G   D7
I saw three ships come sailing in,

|G   Em |C   D7 G
On Christmas Day in the morn - ing.

Verse 2

‖G   D7 |G   D7
And what was in those ships all three?

|G |D7
On Christmas Day, on Christmas Day.

|Em   D7 |G   D7
And what was in those ships all three?

|G   Em |C   D7 G
On Christmas Day in the morn - ing.

Verse 3

‖G   D7 |G   D7
Our Saviour Christ and His la-dy.

|G |D7
On Christmas Day, on Christmas Day.

|Em   D7 |G   D7
Our Saviour Christ and His la-dy.

|G   Em |C   D7 G
On Christmas Day in the morn - ing.

Verse 4

   ‖G   D7 |G   D7
Pray, whither sailed those ships all three?

   |G |D7
On Christmas Day, on Christmas Day.

   |Em   D7 |G   D7
Pray, whither sailed those ships all three?

   |G   Em |C   D7 G
On Christmas Day in the morn - ing.

Verse 5

   ‖G   D7 |G   D7
O, they sailed into Bethle-hem.

   |G |D7
On Christmas Day, on Christmas Day.

   |Em   D7 |G   D7
O, they sailed into Bethle-hem.

   |G   Em |C   D7 G
On Christmas Day in the morn - ing.

Verse 6

   ‖G   D7 |G   D7
And all the bells on earth shall ring,

   |G |D7
On Christmas Day, on Christmas Day.

   |Em D7 |G   D7
And all the bells on earth shall ring,

   |G   Em |C   D7 G
On Christmas Day in the morn - ing.

If I Had a Hammer
(The Hammer Song)

Words and Music by Lee Hays and Pete Seeger

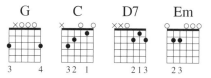

Verse 1

|G |C |G |C
If I had a hammer,   I'd hammer in the morn - ing,

             |G |C |D7 |
I'd hammer in the evening   all over this land,

                |G | |Em |
I'd hammer out danger, I'd hammer out a warning,

                 |C   G |C   G |
I'd hammer out love be - tween my brothers and my sisters,

C   G |D7 |G |C |G |
All   over this land.

Verse 2

‖G |C |G |C
If I had a bell,   I'd ring it in the morn - ing,

             |G |C |D7 |
I'd ring it in the evening   all over this land,

             |G | |Em |
I'd ring out danger, I'd ring out a warning,

             |C   G |C   G |
I'd ring out love be - tween my brothers and my sisters,

C   G |D7 |G |C |G |
All   over this land.

Verse 3

        ‖G |C |G |C
If I had a song,   I'd sing it in the morn - ing,

                |G |C |D7 |
I'd sing it in the evening all over this land,

          |G | |Em |
I'd sing out danger, I'd sing out a warning,

        |C   G |C   G |
I'd sing out love be - tween my brothers and my sisters,

C G|D7 |G |C |G |
All   over this land.

Verse 4

        ‖G |C |G |C
Well, I've got a hammer   and I've got a bell,

           |G |C |D7 |
And I've got a song to sing all over this land,

            |G | |Em |
It's the hammer of justice, it's the bell of freedom,

        |C   G |C   G |
It's the song about love be - tween my brothers and my sisters,

C G|D7 |G |C |G | ‖
All   over this land.

Jamaica Farewell

Words and Music by Irving Burgie

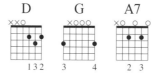

Verse 1

D |G
Down the way where the nights are gay

|A7 |D |
And the moon shines gaily on the mountaintop,

D |G
I took a trip on a sailing ship,

|A7 |D
And when I reached Jamaica, I made a stop.

Chorus

‖D |G |
But I'm sad to say, I'm on my way,

A7 |D
Won't be back for many a day.

|D |G
My heart is down, my head is turning around.

|A7 |D |
I had to leave a little crab in Kingston town.

G |A7 |D   ‖

Verse 2

```
       D                   |G
     Sounds of laughter everywhere,

         |A7                   |D             |
     And the dancing fish swaying to and fro.

       D                   |G
     I must declare my heart is there,

              |A7                    |D
     Though I've been from Maine to Mexico.
```

Repeat Chorus

Verse 3

```
       D                      |G                    |
     Under the sea there you can hear Mer folk

     A7                  |D              |
     Singing songs that I love so dear.

       D                    |G                |A7
     Fish are dancing everywhere and the fun is fine

         |D
     Any time of year.
```

Repeat Chorus

Knock Three Times

Words and Music by
Irwin Levine and Larry Russell Brown

D   A7   G   D7

Verse 1

D
Hey, girl, what ya do-in' down there?

D   **|A7**
Dancin' alone every night while I live right a-bove you.

A7
I can hear your music play-in',

A7
I can feel your body sway-in',

A7   **|D**
One floor below me, you don't even know me, I love you.

Chorus

                          ‖G   **|D**
Oh, my darlin', knock three times on the ceiling if you want me,

A7   **|D |D7**
Twice on the pipe if the answer is no.

                          |G   **|D**
Oh, my sweetness, *(3 knocks)* means you'll meet me in the hallway,

A7   **|D |G A7**
Twice on the pipe means you ain't gonna show.

Verse 2

    ‖**D** | |
If you look out your win-dow tonight,

D | |**A7** | |
Pull in the string with the note that's attached to my heart.

A7 |
Read how many times I saw you,

 |**A7** |
How in my silence I adore you,

 |**A7** | |**D**
And only in my dreams did that wall between us come a-part.

Repeat Chorus (2X)

Knockin' on Heaven's Door

Words and Music by
Bob Dylan

G   D   Am   C

(chord diagrams)

Verse 1

G   D |Am
Mama, take   this badge from me.

G   D |C
I can't use   it any more.

G   D |Am
It's gettin' dark,   too dark to see.

G   D |C
Feels like I'm knockin' on heaven's door.

Chorus

G   D |C
Knock, knock, knockin' on heaven's door.

G   D |C
Knock, knock, knockin' on heaven's door.

G   D |C
Knock, knock, knockin' on heaven's door.

G   D |C
Knock, knock, knockin' on heaven's door.

Verse 2

G   D |Am
Mama, put   my guns in the ground.

G   D |C
I can't shoot   them any more.

G   D |Am
That cold black cloud is comin' down.

G   D |C
Feels like I'm knockin' on heaven's door.

Repeat Chorus (2x)

Kum Ba Yah

Traditional Spiritual

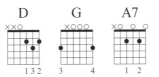

Verse 1

|D   G |D
Kum - bah - yah, my Lord,   Kum - bah - yah,

|D   G   D |A7
Kum - bah - yah, my Lord,   Kum - bah - yah,

D | G |D
Kum - bah - yah, my Lord,   Kum - bah - yah,

A7 |D   A7 |D
Oh, Lord,   Kum - bah - yah.

Verse 2

‖D   G |D
Someone's prayin', Lord,   Kum - bah - yah,

|D   G   D |A7
Someone's prayin', Lord,   Kum - bah - yah,

D | G |D
Someone's prayin', Lord,   Kum - bah - yah,

A7 |D   A7 |D
Oh, Lord,   Kum - bah - yah.

Verse 3

‖D   G |D
Someone's singin', Lord,   Kum - bah - yah,

|D   G   D |A7
Someone's singin', Lord,   Kum - bah - yah,

D | G |D
Someone's singin', Lord,   Kum - bah - yah,

A7 |D   A7 |D   ‖
Oh, Lord,   Kum - bah - yah.

Leaving on a Jet Plane

Words and Music by
John Denver

G   C   D

Verse 1

|**G** |**C**
All my bags are packed, I'm ready to go,

|**G** |**C**
I'm standing here out-side your door,

|**G** |**C** |**D** |
I hate to wake you up to say good-bye.

|**G** |**C**
But the dawn is breakin', it's early morn,

|**G** |**C**
The taxi's waitin', he's blowin' his horn,

|**G** |**C** |**D** |
Al-ready I'm so lonesome I could die.

Chorus

||**G** |**C** |
So kiss me and smile for me,

G |**C** |
Tell me that you'll wait for me,

G |**C** |**D** |
Hold me like you'll never let me go.

|**G** |**C** |**G**
'Cause I'm leavin' on a jet plane,

|**C** |**G**
Don't know when I'll be back again.

|**C** |**D** | | |
Oh, babe, I hate to go.

Verse 2

‖**G** |**C**

There's so many times I've let you down,

|**G** |**C**

So many times I've played around,

|**G** |**C** |**D** |

I tell you now they don't mean a thing.

|**G** |**C**

Every place I go I'll think of you,

|**G** |**C**

Every song I sing I'll sing for you,

|**G** |**C** |**D** |

When I come back I'll bring your wedding ring.

Repeat Chorus

Verse 3

G |**C** |

Now the time has come to leave you,

G |**C**

One more time let me kiss you,

|**G** |**C** |**D** | |

Then close your eyes, I'll be on my way.

G |**C**

Dream about the days to come

|**G** |**C**

When I won't have to leave alone,

|**G** |**C** |**D** | ‖

A-bout the times I won't have to say:

Repeat Chorus

Outro

|**G** |**C** |**G**

I'm leavin' on a jet plane,

|**C** |**G**

Don't know when I'll be back again,

|**C** | |**D** | | | | |**G** ‖

Oh, babe, I hate to go.

Let's Get Together

Words and Music by
Chet Powers

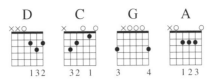

Verse 1

D | | |C | |
Love is but a song we sing, fear's the way we die.

D | | |C | |
You can make the mountains ring or make the angels cry.

D | | |C | ||
Though the bird is on the wing and you may not know why...

Chorus

G |A
Come on people now, smile on your brother.

|D |G A |D | ||
Every-body get together, try to love one an-other right now.

Verse 2

D | | |C | |
Some may come and some may go, we shall surely pass

D | | |C | |
When the one that left us here returns for us at last.

D | | |C | ||
We are but a moment's sunlight fading in the grass.

Repeat Chorus (2X)

Verse 3

D | | |C | |
If you hear the song I sing, we will under-stand.

D | | |C | |
You hold the key to love and fear all in your trembling hand.

D | | |C | ||
Just one key un-locks them both, it's there at your com-mand.

Repeat Chorus

Outro-Chorus

G |A
Come on people now, smile on your brother.

   |D |G   A |D
Every-body get together, try to love one an-other right now,

   |D | | ||
Right now, right now.

Lookin' Out My Back Door

Words and Music by John Fogerty

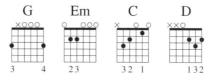

Verse 1

G | |
Just got home from Illinois.

Em | |
Lock the front door, oh boy!

C |**G** |**D** |
Got to sit down, take a rest on the porch.

  |**G** | |
I - magination sets in.

Em | |
Pretty soon I'm singin'.

C |**G** |**D** |**G**
Doo, doo, doo, lookin' out my back door.

Verse 2

      ‖**G** |
There's a giant doing cartwheels,

  |**Em** | |
A statue wearin' high heels.

C |**G** |**D** |
Look at all the happy creatures dancing on the lawn.

  |**G** | |
A dinosaur Vic - trola

Em | |
Listening to Buck Owens.

C |**G** |**D** |**G**   ‖
Doo, doo, doo, lookin' out my back door.

Chorus 1

D |
Tambourines and elephants

  |**C** |**G**
Are playing in the band.

    |**G** |**Em** |**D** | |
Won't you take a ride   on the flyin' spoon? Doo, doo doo.

G |
Wondrous appa - rition

  |**Em** | |
Pro - vided by ma - gician.

C |**G** |**D** |**G**   ‖
Doo, doo, doo, lookin' out my back door.

Chorus 2

D |
Tambourines and elephants

    |**C** |**G**
Are playing in the band.

      |**G** |**Em** |**D** | |
Won't you take a ride   on the flyin' spoon? Doo, doo doo.

G |
Bother me to - morrow.

   |**Em** | |
To - day, I'll buy no sorrows.

C |**G** |**D** |**G** ||
Doo, doo, doo, lookin' out my back door.

Verse 3

G | |
Forward troubles Illinois.

Em | |
Lock the front door, oh boy!

C |**G** |**D** | |
Look at all the happy creatures dancing on the lawn.

G |
Bother me to - morrow.

   |**Em** | |
To - day, I'll buy no sorrows.

C |**G** |**D** |**G** ||
Doo, doo, doo, lookin' out my back door.

Ode to Billy Joe

Words and Music by
Bobbie Gentry

D7   G7   C7

| |

Verse 1

|D7
It was the third of June,
|D7
Another sleepy, dusty Delta day.
|D7
I was out choppin' cotton
|D7
And my brother was balin' hay.
|G7
And at dinner time we stopped
|G7
And walked back to the house to eat,
|D7
And Mama hollered out the back door,
|D7
"Y'all re - member to wipe your feet."
|G7
And then she said, "I got some news this morn - in'
|G7
From Choctaw Ridge.
|D7
Today Billy Joe McAllister
|C7 |D7
Jumped off the Tallahatchie Bridge."

Verse 2

‖**D7**
And Papa said to Mama

|**D7** | |
As he passed around the black-eyed peas,

|**D7** |
"Well, Billy Joe   never had a lick o' sense.

D7 | |
Pass the biscuits, please.

|**G7**
There's five more acres

|**G7** | |
In the lower forty I've got to plow."

|**D7**
And Mama said it was shame

|**D7** | |
About   Billy Joe, anyhow.

|**G7**
Seems like nothin' ever comes

|**G7** | |
To no good   up on Choctaw Ridge.

|**D7**
And now Billy Joe McAllister's

|**C7** |**D7** |
Jumped off the Tallahatchie Bridge.

Verse 3

‖**D7**
And Brother said he recollected
　　|**D7**　　　　　　　　　　　　　|　　　　　　　　　|
When he and Tom and Billie Joe
　　|**D7**
Put a frog down my back
　　|**D7**　　　　　　　　　|　　　　　　　　|
At the Carroll County picture show.
　　　　|**G7**
And wasn't I talkin' to him
　|**G7**　　　　　　　　|　　　　　　　|
After church last Sunday night?
　　　|**D7**　　　　　　　　　　|
I'll have an - other piece of apple pie.
D7　　　　　　　　　|　　　　　　|
　　You know, it don't seem right.
|**G7**　　　　　　　　　|
I saw him at the sawmill yester - day
　　　　|**G7**　　　　|
On Choctaw Ridge.
　　　|**D7**
And now you tell me Billie Joe's
　|**C7**　　　　　　　|**D7**　　　　　|　　　　　‖
Jumped off the Tallahatchie Bridge.

Verse 4

D7
Mama said to me,
    |D7 | |
"Child, what's happened to your appetite?
    |D7
I've been cookin' all morning
    |D7 | |
And you haven't touched a single bite.
  |G7
That nice young preacher,
    |G7 | |
Brother Taylor, dropped by today.
       |D7
Said he'd be pleased to have dinner
  |D7 | |
On Sunday. Oh, by the way,
  |G7 |
He said he saw a girl that looked a lot like you
        |G7 |
Up on Choctaw Ridge,
    |D7
And she and Billy Joe was throwing
  |C7   **|D7** |
Somethin' off the Tallahatchie Bridge."

Verse 5

||**D7**
A year has come and gone

|**D7**
Since we heard the news 'bout Billy Joe.

|**D7**
And Brother married Becky Thompson;

|**D7**
They bought a store in Tupelo.

|**G7**
There was a virus goin' 'round,

|**G7**
Papa caught it and he died last spring.

|**D7**
And now Mama doesn't seem

|**D7**
To wanna do much of anything.

|**G7**
And me, I spend a lot of time pickin' flowers up

|**G7**
On Choctaw Ridge

|**D7**
And drop them into the muddy water

C7 |**D7**
Off the Tallahatchie Bridge.

65

Louisiana Bayou

Words and Music by
Dave Matthews Band and Mark Batson

A   Dm/F   A/E   A/C#

1 2 3   3 2 4 1   1 2 3   3 1

Verse 1

A
No, no, Mama cried devil; they do - si - do.

A
Two young boys lyin' dead by the side of the road.

A
The coins on their eyes represent the mon - ey they owe.

A
No judge or jury ever gonna hear the story told.

Chorus 1

‖**A**
Down by the bayou,

|**A**
Try'n' to play with the cane, you, ah.

|**A**
Try'n' to play with the cane, you, ah.

|**A**
Same story again, you, ah.

|**A**
Down by the bayou,

|**A**
Try'n' to play with the cane, you, ah.

|**A**
Try'n' to play with the cane, you, ah.

|**A**
Same story again, you.

|**A**
Louisiana Bayou.

Verse 2

A

Sweet girl, Daddy done beat that girl like he's insane.

A

Brother can't watch him beat that girl down again.

A

Till late one night cookin' up with a cou - ple of friends,

A

Swears his daddy never gonna see an - other day.

‖A

Chorus 2

Down by the bayou,

|A

Try'n' to play with the cane,   you, ah.

|A

Try'n' to play with the cane,   you, ah.

|A

Same story again,   you, ah.

|A

Down by the bayou,

|A

Try'n' to play with the cane,   you, ah.

|A

Try'n' to play with the cane,   you, ah.

|A

Same story again,   you, ah.

Bridge

||**A** | |

Bring the same. No, no, Mama cried devil; they do - si - do.

A |

  See two young boys lyin' dead by the side of the road.

|**A**   **Dm/F**

Shame, shame.

|**Dm/F**   **A/E** | **A/C♯** |

Oh, it's a shame to lose your   way running wild.

A/C♯   **A** |

It's a shame to lose your… Shame, shame.

Dm/F | **A/E** | **A/C♯** |

Oh, it's a shame to lose your way as a child.   Oh,   oh,

A/C♯   **A** ||

  It's a shame to lose your…

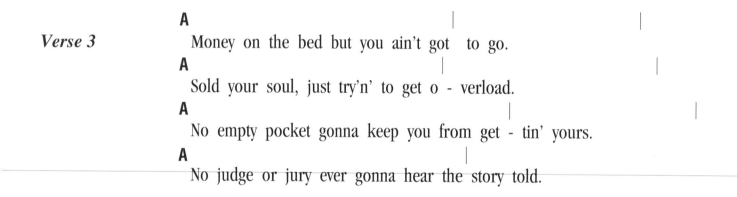

Verse 3

A | |

  Money on the bed but you ain't got to go.

A | |

  Sold your soul, just try'n' to get o - verload.

A | |

  No empty pocket gonna keep you from get - tin' yours.

A |

  No judge or jury ever gonna hear the story told.

Repeat Chorus 2

Outro

A

No, no, Mama cried devil; they do - si - do.

A

Two young boys lyin' dead by the side of the road.

|A

Down by the bayou,

|A

Try'n' to play with the cane, you, ah.

|A

Try'n' to play with the cane, you, ah.

|A

Same story again, you, ah.

|A

Down by the bayou,

Dm/F

Try'n' to play with the cane, you, ah.

A/E

Try'n' to play with the cane, you, ah.

A/C♯   A

Same story again, you, ah.

|A

Down by the bayou,

|A

Louisiana Bayou.

|A

Louisiana Bayou.

Man of Constant Sorrow

Traditional

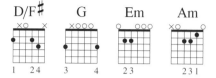

Verse 1

|D/F♯ | |G |
I am a man   of constant sorrow,

|Em | |Am |
I've seen trou - ble all my days.

|D/F♯ | |G |
I bid fare - well   to old Ken - tucky,

|Em | |Am |
The place where I   was born and raised.

Verse 2

‖D/F♯ | |G |
For six long years   I've been in trouble,

|Em | |Am |
No pleasure here   on earth I've found.

|D/F♯ | |G |
For in this world   I'm bound to ramble,

|Em | |Am |
I have no friends   to help me now.

Verse 3

```
            ‖D/F♯   |                |G      |
It's fare you well,      my own true lover,

          |Em   |              |Am   |
I never ex - pect    to see you a - gain.

             |D/F♯  |              |G
For I'm bound to ride      that northern railroad,

          |Em   |            |Am   |
Perhaps I'll die      upon this train.
```

Verse 4

```
            ‖D/F♯  |               |G      |
You can bury me       in some deep valley,

          |Em     |              |Am   |
For many years       where I may lay,

             |D/F♯  |              |G      |
Then you may learn      to love an - other,

          |Em     |            |Am   |
While I am sleep - ing in my grave.
```

Verse 5

```
            ‖D/F♯    |                 |G      |
Maybe your friends    think I'm just a stranger,

          |Em   |              |Am    |
My face you nev  -  er will see no more,

             |D/F♯  |              |G      |
But there is one       promise that is given,

          |Em   |            |Am   |    ‖
I'll meet you on    God's golden shore.
```

Me and Bobby McGee

Words and Music by
Kris Krisofferson and Fred Foster

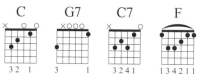

Verse 1

C
Busted flat in Baton Rouge,   headin' for the trains,

C   **G7**
Feelin' nearly faded as my jeans.

G7
       Bobby thumbed a diesel down   just before it rained,

G7   **C**
       Took us all the way to New Orleans.

C
I took my har - poon out of my dirty red ban - dana

              C   **C7**   **F**
And was blowin' sad while Bobby sang the blues.

              F   **C**
With them windshield wipers slappin' time and Bobby clappin' hands,

       G7   **C**
We finally sang up every song that driver knew.

Chorus 1

F   **C**
       Freedom's just an - other word for nothin' left to lose.

G7   **C**
       Nothin' ain't worth nothin', but it's free.

F   **C**
       Feelin' good was easy, Lord, when   Bobby sang the blues,

G7
       And feelin' good was good enough for me,

G7   **C**
       Good enough for me and Bobby Mc - Gee.

Verse 2

||**C** | | | |
From the coal mines of Ken - tucky   to the California sun,

C | |**G7** | |
Bobby shared the secrets of my soul.

G7 | | | |
     Standin' right be - side me, Lord, through   everything I done,

G7 | |**C** |
     And every night she kept me from the cold.

|**C** | | | |
Then somewhere near Sa - linas, Lord, I let her slip a - way,

C |**C7** |**F** |
Lookin' for the home I hope she'll find.

|**F** | |**C** | |
And I'd trade all of my to - morrows for a single yester - day,

G7 | |**C** | ||
Holdin' Bobby's body next to mine.

Chorus 2

F | |**C** | |
     Freedom's just an - other word for nothin' left to lose.

G7 | |**C** | |
     Nothin' left is all she left for me.

F | |**C** | |
     Feelin' good was easy, Lord, when   Bobby sang the blues,

G7 | | | |
     And, buddy, that was good enough for me,

G7 | |**C** | ||
     Good enough for me and Bobby Mc - Gee.

MMM Bop

Words and Music by
Isaac Hanson, Taylor Hanson and Zac Hanson

A   E   D

123   231   132

Verse 1

A   E |D
You have so many re - lationships in this life,

     E |A
Only one or two will last.

           E |D
You're going through all this pain and strife,

          E |A E
Then you turn your back and they're gone so fast,

    |D E |A   E |D E ||
Ooh yeah,   and they're gone so fast.

Verse 2

A   E |D
So hold on to the ones who really care,

     E |A
In the end they'll be the only ones there.

       E |D
When you get old and start losing your hair,

   E |A   E |D
Can you tell me who will still care?

   E |A   E |D E ||
Can you tell me who will still care? Oh, oh, yeah, yeah.

Chorus

A |D
Mmm bop, ba du-ba dop, ba du bop, ba du-ba dop.

 |A |E |
Ba du bop, ba du-ba dop, ba du, yah-ee, yeah.

A |D
Mmm bop, ba du-ba dop, ba du bop, ba du-ba dop.

 |A |E ||
Ba du bop, ba du-ba dop, ba du, yah-ee, yeah.

Verse 3

```
         A                E                       |D
      Plant a seed, plant a flower, plant a rose.

              E                     |A
      You can plant any one of those.

            E                          |D
      Keep planting to find out which one grows.

          E          |A     E |D
      It's a secret no one  knows,

          E          |A     E |D E          ||
      It's a secret no one  knows,    no  one knows.
```

Repeat Chorus

Bridge

```
      A    E                    |D   E                    |A
       In an mmm bop they're gone, in an mmm bop they're not there.

            E                    |D   E                   |A E |D
      In an mmm bop they're gone, in an mmm bop they're not there

           E              |A   E          |D              E              ||
      Un-til you lose your hair, uh  huh, but you don't care, mmm  yeah, yeah.
```

Repeat Chorus

Outro

```
      A        E    |D           E                |A
       Can you tell me? Uh,  you know you can, but you don't know.

              E      |D              E                |A
      Can you tell me? Oh yeah, you say you can, but you don't know.

              E      |D              E                |A
      Can you tell me? Ah,  you know you can, but you don't know.

              E    |D          E                  |A E |D
      Can you tell me?  You say you can, but you don't know.

            E                    |A
      You say you can, but you don't know,

      E                |D       E ||
      You don't know, you don't know.
```

Repeat Chorus

My Generation

Words and Music by
Peter Townshend

```
   A          G          D/A
  x o     o  x o o o    x o o
 ● ● ●      ●       ●   ● ● ●
  1 2 3    3       4     1 3 2
```

Intro   A |G |A |G ||

Verse 1
                   A |G |
People try to put us d - down.
                   A   D/A |G |
(Talkin' 'bout my generation.)
                   A |G |
   Just because we   get around.
                   A   D/A |G |
(Talkin' 'bout my generation.)
                   A |G |
Things they do look awful c - c - cold.
                   A   D/A |G
(Talkin' 'bout my generation.)
                   |A |G |
I hope I die before   I get old.
                   A   D/A |G
(Talkin' 'bout my generation.)
                             |A |G
This is my gener - ation.
                             |A |G ||
This is my gener - ation, baby.

Verse 2

```
        A                   |G        |
        Why don't you all f - fade away?
        A     D/A  |G         |
(Talkin' 'bout my generation.)
        A                   |G        |
Don't try to dig what we all s - s - say.
        A     D/A  |G
(Talkin' 'bout my generation.)
          |A                  |G       |A
I'm not tryin' to cause a big  s - s - sensa - tion.
             D/A   |G
(Talkin' 'bout my generation.)
          |A            |G           |A
I'm just talkin' 'bout my g - g - g - gener - ation.
             D/A   |G
(Talkin' 'bout my generation.)
                        |A          |G
This is my gener - ation.
                        |A          |G           ||
This is my gener - ation, baby.
```

Repeat Verse 1

My Ramblin' Boy

Words and Music by Tom Paxton

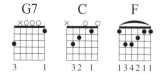

Verse 1

   |G7 |C
He was a man and a friend al - ways,

            |G7 |C
He stuck with me in the hard old days.

       |C |
He never cared if I had no dough,

         |G7 |C
We rambled 'round in the rain and snow.

Chorus

          ||C   F |C
And here's to you my ramblin' boy,

         |G7 |C
May all your ramblin' bring you joy.

        |C   F |C
And here's to you my ramblin' boy,

        |G7 |C
May all your ramblin' bring you joy.

Verse 2

```
       ‖G7                  |C
In Tulsa town we chanced to stray.

              |G7           |C
We thought we'd try to work one day.

              |C                 |
The boss said he had room for one.

              |G7          |C
Says my old pal, "We'd rather bum!"
```

Repeat Chorus

Verse 3

```
       ‖G7              |C
Late one night in a jungle camp,

              |G7           |C
The weather it was cold and damp.

              |C                    |
He got the chills and he got 'em bad;

              |G7         |C      ‖
They took the only friend I had.
```

Repeat Chorus

Verse 4

```
       ‖G7              |C
He left me there to ramble on,

              |G7            |C
My ramblin' pal is dead and gone.

              |C                 |
If when we die, we go some - where,

              |G7             |C    ‖
I'll bet you a dollar, he's ramblin' there.
```

Repeat Chorus

Oh! Susanna

Words and Music by Stephen C. Foster

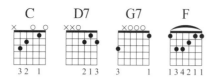

Verse

|C | |D7 |G7
I come from Ala - bama with a banjo on my knee.

|C | |G7 |C
I'm goin' to Lou'si - ana, my Su - sanna for to see.

|C | |D7 |G7
It rained all night the day I left, the weather it was dry.

|C | |G7 |C ||
The sun so hot I froze to death. Su - sanna, don't you cry.

Chorus

F | |C D7 |G7
Oh, Su - sanna, oh don't you cry for me,

|C | |G7 |C ||
For I come from Ala - bama with a banjo on my knee.

Rodeo Clowns

Words and Music by Jack Johnson

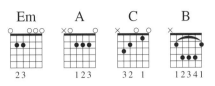

Verse 1

Em
Sweeping the floors, open up the doors, yeah.

A
Turn on the lights, getting ready for tonight.

C
Nobody's romancing 'cause it's too early for dancing,

|B
But here comes the music.

Verse 2

Em
Bright lights flashing to cover up your lack of soul.

|A
Man - y people, so many problems,

|C
So many reasons to buy an - other round; drink it down.

|B
Just another night on the town

|Em
With the big man, money man, better than the other man.

A
He got the plan with the million dollar give a damn.

C
When nobody understands he'll become a smaller man.

|B
The bright lights keep flashing.

Chorus

                                        ‖**Em**   **B**
Women keep on dancing with the clowns, yeah, yeah, yeah.

                                 |**C**   **A**
They pick me up when I'm down,   yeah, yeah.

                |**Em**   **B**
The rodeo clowns,   yeah, yeah, yeah,

                           |**C**   **A**   ‖
They pick me up when I'm down.

Verse 3

       ‖**Em**
The disco ball spinning,

                               |**A**
All the music and the women and the shots of tequila.

Man, they say that they need ya.

  |**C**
But what they really need

     |**B**
Is just a little room to breathe.

     |**Em**
Teeny bopping disco queen,

                      |**A**
She barely understands her dreams   of bellybutton rings

                  |**C**
And other kinds of things sym - bolic of change.

But the thing that is strange

  |**B**
Is that the changes occurred.

Chorus

               ‖**Em**   **B**
And now she's just a part of the herd, yeah, yeah, yeah.

             |**C**   **A**
Man, I thought that you heard, yeah, yeah.

       |**Em**   **B**
The changes occurred, yeah, yeah, yeah.

        |**C**   **A**   ‖
Just a part of the herd.

Verse 4

Em |
Lights out, shut down, late night, wet ground.

A |
 You walk by, look at him, but he can't look at you, yeah.

C |
 You might feel pity, but he only feels the ground.

B |
 You understand moods, but he only knows letdown.

Em |
  By the corner there's another one

A |
Reaching out a hand, coming from a broken man.

    |**C** |**B**
Well, you try to live, but he's done trying. Not dead,

Chorus

       ‖**Em**
But definitely dying

B |**C**   **A**
 With the rest of the clowns, yeah, yeah.

        |**Em**   **B**
Mm, mm, mm, mm, mm, mm, mm,

          |**C**   **A**   ‖
With the rest of the clowns.

Repeat Verse 1

Ring of Fire

Words and Music by
Merle Kilgore and June Carter

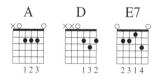

A   D   E7

Verse 1

A | **D** |**A** |**D** |**A** |
Love   is a burning thing

|**A** | **E7** |**A** |**E7** |**A** | |
And it makes   a fiery ring.

A | **D** |**A** |**D** |**A** | |
Bound   by wild de-sires,

A |**E7** |**A** | ||
I fell into a ring of fire.

Chorus

E7 | |**D** |**A**
I   fell   in - to a burning ring of fire.

|**E7** | |**D** |**A**
I went down,   down,   down,   and the flames   went   higher.

|**A** | | **E7** |**A** |
And it burns,   burns,   burns,   the ring of fire,

E7 |**A** |
The ring of fire.

Verse 2

```
    ||A            |      D    |A          |D    |A              |
    The  taste         of  love  is  sweet

        |A         |        E7  |A       |E7   |A         |            |
    When  hearts         like  ours  meet.

    A          |D   |A     |      D    |A    |      |
    I  fell  for  you  like  a  child

    A         |        E7    |A      |              ||
    Oh,          but  the  fire  went  wild.
```

Repeat Chorus

Tag

```
        ||A              |            |      E7   |A          |
    And  it  burns,    burns,    burns,      the  ring  of  fire,

        E7    |A        |      E7   |A        ||
    The  ring  of  fire,      the  ring  of  fire.
```

Sexy Plexi

Words and Music by Jack Johnson

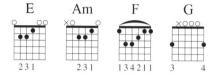

Verse 1

E |**Am** |
Sexy, sexy, made up of plexi dis - asters.

E |
Pushing and pulling, conservative rolling,

Am |
Unlike plastic, easier to see through,

E |
Just like glass with no ring,

Am |
Softer and sadder you sing.

E |
Sexy, sexy, do your thing,

Am |
Learn to be shy and then you can sting.

E |
Plexi, plexi, bend, don't shatter.

F   **G**   ‖
Once you're broken, shape won't matter.

Chorus

<pre>
    Am   G
      You're breaking your   mind

    |F   E
By killing the time that kills   you.

    |Am   G
But you can't blame the time,

                  |F   E |Am | ‖
'Cause it's on - ly in your mind.
</pre>

Verse 2

<pre>
    E
Quickly, quickly grow and then you'll know

              |Am
It's such an awkward show to see.

    |E
And everyone you wanted to know

    |Am
And everyone you wanted to meet

          |E |Am
Have all   gone away.

                      |E |F   G   ‖
Well, they've all   gone away.   And now…
</pre>

Repeat Chorus

Bridge

<pre>
    Am |E
      You're breaking your mind, you're   breaking your mind.

    |Am |E
You're   breaking your mind, you're   breaking your mind.

    |Am |E
You're   breaking your mind, you're   breaking your mind.

    |Am |E |F   G   ‖
You're   breaking your mind, you're   breaking your mind, mind,   mind.
</pre>

Outro

<pre>
Am   G |F   E |Am   G |F   E |Am   ‖
</pre>

Shelter from the Storm

Words and Music by Bob Dylan

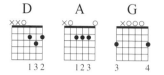

Verse 1

D |A |G |D
'Twas in another lifetime, one of toil and blood,

 |D |A |G | |
When blackness was a virtue and the road was full of mud.

D |A |G |
I came in from the wilderness, a creature void of form.

 |D |A |G |D |A |G |D
"Come in," she said, "I'll give you shelter from the storm."

Verse 2

 ||D |A |G |D
And if I pass this way again, you can rest as - sured

 |D |A |G |
I'll always do my best for her, on that I give my word,

 |D |A |G |
In a world of steel-eyed death, and men who are fighting to be warm.

 |D |A |G |D |A |G |D |
"Come in," she said, "I'll give you shelter from the storm."

Verse 3

```
 ‖D                          |A                 |G            |D          |
Not a word was spoke be - tween us; there was little risk in - volved.
 D            |A            |G           |        |
   Everything up to that point had been left unre - solved.
 D            |A           |G          |
   Try imagin - ing a place where it's always safe and warm.
         |D              |A    |G         |D    |A    |G    |D    |
"Come in," she said, "I'll give you shelter from the storm."
```

Verse 4

```
 ‖D                      |A    |G         |D          |
I was burned out from ex - haustion, buried in the hail,
 D                |A       |G          |        |
   Poisoned in the bushes an' blown out on the trail,
 D            |A      |G        |
   Hunted like a crocodile, ravaged in the corn.
         |D              |A    |G         |D    |A    |G    |D    ‖
"Come in," she said, "I'll give you shelter from the storm."
```

Verse 5

```
 D            |A                 |G           |D
   Suddenly I turned around and she was standin' there
   |D             |A              |G          |
With silver bracelets on her wrists and flowers in her hair.
   |D              |A            |G              |
She walked up to me so gracefully and took my crown of thorns.
         |D              |A    |G         |D    |A    |G    |D
"Come in," she said, "I'll give you shelter from the storm."
```

Verse 6

```
 ‖D                     |A    |G              |D
Now there's a wall be - tween us; somethin' there's been lost.
 |D             |A      |G          |        |
I took too much for granted; I got my signals crossed.
 D                |A         |G           |
Just to think that it all began on a non-eventful morn.
         |D              |A    |G         |D    |A    |G    |D
"Come in," she said, "I'll give you shelter from the storm."
```

Verse 7

        ‖D |A |G |D
Well, the deputy walks on hard nails and the preacher rides a mount,

    |D |A |G |
But nothing really matters much; it's doom alone that counts.

       |D |A |G |
And the one-eyed under - taker, he blows a futile horn.

      |D |A |G |D |A |G |D ‖
"Come in," she said, "I'll give you shelter from the storm."

Verse 8

   D |A |G |D |
I've heard newborn babies wailin' like a mournin' dove

  |D |A |G |
And old men with broken teeth stranded without love.

  |D |A |G |
Do I understand your question, man? Is it hopeless and for - lorn?

   |D |A |G |D |A |G |D
"Come in," she said, "I'll give you shelter from the storm."

Verse 9

   ‖D |A |G |D
In a little hilltop village, they gambled for my clothes.

 |D |A |G |
I bargained for sal - vation an' she gave me a lethal dose.

 |D |A |G |
I offered up my innocence and got repaid with scorn.

  |D |A |G |D |A |G |D
"Come in," she said, "I'll give you shelter from the storm."

Verse 10

   ‖D |A |G |D |
Well, I'm livin' in a foreign country but I'm bound to cross the line.

D |A |G |
Beauty walks a razor's edge; some - day I'll make it mine.

   |D |A |G |
If I could only turn back the clock to when God and her were born.

   |D |A |G |D |A |G |D ‖
"Come in," she said, "I'll give you shelter from the storm."

This Land Is Your Land

Words and Music by Woody Guthrie

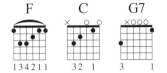

Chorus

‖**F** | **C** |
This land is your land and this land is my land,

|**G7** | **C** |
From Cali - fornia to the New York Island,

|**F** | **C** | |
From the redwood forest to the Gulf Stream waters,

G7 | **C** |
This land was made for you and me.

Verse 1

‖**F** |**C** |
As I was walking that ribbon of highway,

|**G7** | **C** |
I saw a - bove me that endless skyway.

|**F** | **C** | |
I saw be - low me that golden valley,

G7 | **C** |
This land was made for you and me.

Repeat Chorus

Verse 2
                ‖F | **|C** |
I've roamed and rambled and I followed my footsteps

            |G7 | **|C** |
To the sparkling sands of her diamond deserts.

        |F | **|C** | |
All a-round me, a voice was sounding,

G7 | **|C** |
"This land was made for you and me."

Repeat Chorus

Verse 3
                ‖F | **|C** |
When the sun came shining and I was strolling,

            |G7 | **|C** |
And the wheat fields waving and the dust clouds rolling,

           |F | **|C** | |
As the fog was lifting a voice was chanting,

G7 | **|C** |
"This land was made for you and me."

Repeat Chorus

Verse 4
                  ‖**F** | |**C** |
In the shadow of the steeple I saw my people,

           |**G7** | |**C** |
By the relief office I seen my people.

               |**F** | |**C** | |
As they stood there hungry, I stood there asking,

G7 | |**C** |
"Is this land made for you and me?"

Repeat Chorus

Verse 5
                  ‖**F** | |**C** | |
Nobody living can ever stop me

        |**G7** | |**C** |
As I go walking down that freedom highway,

        |**F** | |**C** | |
Nobody living can ever make me turn back.

G7 | |**C** | ‖
This land was made for you and me.

Silent Night

Words by Joseph Mohr
Translated by John F. Young
Music by Franz X. Gruber

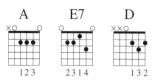

Verse 1

A
Silent night, holy night!

E7   **A**
All is calm, all is bright.

D   **A**
Round yon virgin Mother and Child.

D   **A**
Holy Infant, so tender and mild,

E7   **A**
Sleep in heavenly peace.

A   **E7**   **A**
Sleep in heavenly peace.

Verse 2

A
Silent night, holy night!

E7   **A**
Shepherds quake at the sight.

D   **A**
Glories stream from heaven afar.

D   **A**
Heav'nly hosts sing Alleluia,

E7   **A**
Christ, the Savior, is born.

A   **E7**   **A**
Christ, the Savior, is born.

Verse 3

A | |
Silent night, holy night!

E7 |**A** |
Son of God, love's pure light.

D |**A** |
Radiant beams from Thy holy face,

D |**A** |
With the dawn of re-deeming grace,

E7 |**A** |
Jesus, Lord at Thy birth.

A   **E7** |**A** ||
Jesus, Lord at Thy birth.

So You Want to Be a Rock and Roll Star

Words and Music by
Roger McGuinn and Chris Hillman

G | A | D | E

Verse 1

G A | G A
So you want to be a rock and roll star.
|G A |G A |
Then listen now to what I say.
G A |G A
Just get an elec - tric gui - tar
|G A |G A |
And take some time and learn how to play.
D |E
And with your hair swung right
|A |D ||
And your pants too tight, it's gonna be all right.

Verse 2

G A |G A
Then it's time to go down - town,
|G A |G A |
Where the agent man won't let you down.
G A |G A
Sell your soul to the compa - ny
|G A |G A |
Who are waiting there to sell plastic-ware.
D |E
And in a week or two
|A |D ||
If you make the charts, the girls'll tear you apart.

Verse 3

```
         G              A           |G        A
          The price you paid for your riches and fame,
         |G         A              |G      A                    |
Was it all a strange   game? You're a little in - sane.
         G              A          |G         A
          The money that came and the public ac - claim,
             |G         A          |G          A          |
Don't for - get what you are; you're a rock and roll   star.
         D         |E
          La la la la la la
            |A           |D                      ||
La la la la la la la la la la.
```

Teach Your Children

Words and Music by Graham Nash

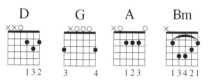

Verse 1

D |**G**
You who are on the road

|**D** |**A**
Must have a code that you can live by.

|**D** |**G**
And so become your - self,

|**D** |**A** ||
Because the past is just a goodbye.

Chorus 1

D |**G**
Teach your children well,

|**D** |**A**
Their father's hell did slowly go by.

|**D** |**G**
And feed them on your dreams,

|**D** |**A** |
The one they pick's the one you'll know by.

D |**G**
Don't you ever ask them why,

|**D**
If they told you, you would cry,

|**Bm** |**G**   **A**
So just look at them and sigh

|**D** |**G**   **D** |**A**
And know they love you.

Verse 2

    ‖**D** |**G**
And you, of the tender years

          |**D** |**A**
Can't know the fears that your elders grew by.

        |**D** |**G**
And so please help them with your youth,

        |**D** |**A**   ‖
They seek the truth before they can die.

Chorus 2

D |**G**
Teach your parents well,

        |**D** |**A**
Their children's hell did slowly go by.

   |**D** |**G**
And feed them on your dreams,

      |**D** |**A**
The one they pick's the one you'll know by.

D |**G**
  Don't you ever ask them why,

            |**D**
If they told you, you would cry,

         |**Bm** |**G**   **A**
So just look at them and sigh

       |**D** |**G** |**D** **A** |**D**   ‖
And know they love you.

Three Little Birds

Words and Music by
Bob Marley

A   D   E

1 2 3   1 3 2   2 3 1

Intro   A | | |

Chorus
‖A |
Don't worry about a thing,
|D |A
'Cause every little thing gonna be all right.
|A |
Singin', "Don't worry about a thing,
|D |A
'Cause every little thing gonna be all right."

Verse
‖A |E
Rise up this morning, smiled with the rising sun.
|A |D
Three little birds   pitch by my doorstep,
|A |E
Singin' sweet   songs of melodies pure and true,
|D   A |
Sayin', "This is my message to you-ou-ou."   Singin',

Repeat Chorus

Repeat Verse

Repeat Chorus (2x)

Wild Montana Skies

Words and Music by
John Denver

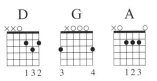

Verse 1

|D | |G |D |
He was born in the Bitterroot Valley in the early mornin' rain,

D | | |A
Wild geese over the wa-ter headin' north and home again,

|D | |G |D
Bringin' a warm wind from the south, bringin' the first taste of the spring,

|D | |A |D |
His mother took him to her breast and softly she did sing:

Chorus 1

||G |A |D |
Oh, oh, Mon-tana, give this child a home,

|G |A |D |
Give him the love of a good family and a woman of his own,

|G |A |D |G
Give him a fire in his heart, give him a light in his eyes,

|D | |A | |D | |G A |D
Give him the wild wind for a broth-er and the wild Montana skies.

Verse 2

||D | |G |D
His mother died that summer, he never learned to cry.

|D | | |A
He never knew his fa-ther, he never did ask why.

|D | |G |D
And he never knew the an-swers that would make an easy way,

|D | |A |D |
But he learned to know the wil-derness and to be a man that way.

Verse 3

    ‖D | |G |D
His mother's brother took him in to his family and his home,

         |D | | |A
Gave him a hand   that he could lean on and a strength to call his own,

      |D | |G |D
And he learned to be a farm-er and he learned to love the land,

      |D | |A |D |
And he learned to read the sea-sons and he learned to make a stand.

Repeat Chorus 1

Verse 4

    ‖D | |G |D
On the eve of his twenty-first birthday he set out on his own.

      |D | | |A
He was thirty years and runnin' when he found his way back home,

        |D | |G |D
Ridin' a storm   across the moun-tains and an ach - in' in his heart,

      |D | |A |D |
Said he came to turn the pag-es and to make   a brand-new start.

Verse 5

    ‖D | |G |D
Now he never told the story of the time that he was gone,

      |D | | |A
Some say he was a law-yer, some say he was a john.

      |D | |G |D
There was somethin' in the cit-y that he said he couldn't breathe,

      |D | |A |D |
And there was somethin' in the coun-try that he said he couldn't leave.

Repeat Chorus 1

Verse 6
‖D | |G |D
Now some say he was crazy, some are glad he's gone,

|D | | |A
But some of us will miss him and we'll try to carry on,

|D | |G |D
Giving a voice to the for-est, giving a voice to the dawn,

|D | |A |D |
Giving a voice to the wil-derness and the land that he lived on.

Chorus 2
‖G |A |D |
Oh, oh, Mon-tana, give this child a home,

|G |A |D |
Give him the love of a good family and a woman of his own,

|G |A |D |G
Give him a fire in his heart, give him a light in his eyes,

|D | |A | |D |
Give him the wild wind for a broth-er and the wild Montana skies.

Outro-Chorus
‖G |A |D |
Oh, oh, Mon-tana, give this child a home,

|G |A |D |
Give him the love of a good family and a woman of his own,

|G |A |D |G
Give him a fire in his heart, give him a light in his eyes,

|D | |
Give him the wild wind for a broth-er and the

A | | | |D | |G A|D ‖
Wild Montana skies.

Tom Dooley

Traditional Folksong

D   A

Verse 1

D | |
Hang your head, Tom Dooley,

D |**A** |
Hang your head and cry.

A |
Killed poor Laura Fos - ter.

  |**A** |**D**
You know you bound to die.

Verse 2

  ‖**D** |
You took her on the hillside,

  |**D** |**A**
As God Almighty knows.

  |**A** |
You took her on the hillside,

  |**A** |**D**
And there you hid her clothes.

Verse 3

   ‖ **D** |
You took her on the roadside,

          |**D** |**A** |
Where you begged to be ex - cused.

    |**A** |
You took her by the roadside,

     |**A** |**D**
Where there you hid her shoes.

Verse 4

   ‖ **D** |
You took her on the hillside

    |**D** |**A** |
To make her be your wife.

    |**A** |**A**
You took her on the hillside,

     |**A** |**D**   ‖
Where there you took her life.

Twist and Shout

Words and Music by
Bert Russell and Phil Medley

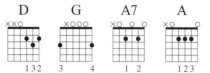

Chorus

|D   G |A7
Well, shake it up, ba - by, now, (Shake it up, ba - by.)

|D   G |A7
Twist and shout. (Twist and shout.)

|D   G |A7
Come on, come on, come on, come on, baby, now, (Come on, ba - by.)

|D G |A7
Come on and work it on out. (Work it on out.)

Verse 1

‖D G |A7
Well, work it on out. (Work it on out.)

|D   G |A7
You know you look so good. (Look so good.)

|D   G |A7
You know you got me goin', now, (Got me goin'.)

|D   G |A7
Just like I knew you would. (Like I knew you would, oo.)

Repeat Chorus

Verse 2   ‖**D G** |**A7**
You know you twist, little girl,   (Twist little girl.)

          |**D**   **G** |**A7**
You know you twist so fine. (Twist so fine.)

                    |**D**   **G** |**A7**
Come on and twist a little closer, now, (Twist a little closer.)

                    |**D**   **G** |**A7**   ‖
And let me know that you're mine. (Let me know you're mine,   oo.)

            A | | |**A7** | |
Interlude   Ah, ah, ah,   ah, wow!

Repeat Chorus

Repeat Verse 2

                        ‖**D**   **G** |**A7**
Outro   Well, shake it, shake it, shake it, baby, now. (Shake it up, ba - by.)

            |**D**   **G** |**A7**
Well, shake it, shake it, shake it, baby, now. (Shake it up, ba - by.)

            |**D**   **G** |**A7** |
Well, shake it, shake it, shake it, baby, now. (Shake it up, ba - by.)

A | | |**A7** |**D**   ‖
Ah, ah, ah, ah.

Up on the Housetop

Words and Music by B.R. Handy

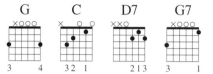

Verse 1

G | |
Up on the housetop reindeer pause,

C   **G** |**D7** |
Out jumps good old Santa Claus.

G | |
Down through the chimney with lots of toys,

C   **G** |**D7**   **G** ||
All for the little ones, Christmas joys.

Chorus

C |**G** |
Ho, ho, ho, who wouldn't go?

D7 |**G** |
Ho, ho, ho, who wouldn't go?

G   **G7** |**C** |
Up on the house-top, click, click, click.

G |**D7**   **G** ||
Down through the chimney with good Saint Nick.

Verse 2

```
G                          |              |
First comes the stocking of little Nell,

C       G    |D7          |
Oh, dear Santa, fill it well.

G                      |                    |
Give her a dollie that laughs and cries,

C            G      |D7      G    ||
One that will open and shut her eyes.
```

Repeat Chorus

Verse 3

```
G                          |              |
Next comes the stocking of little Will,

C      G        |D7            |
Oh, just see what a glorious fill!

G                   |              |
Here is a hammer and lots of tacks,

C    G        |D7      G    ||
Also a ball and a whip that cracks.
```

Repeat Chorus

Will the Circle Be Unbroken

Words by Ada R. Habershon
Music by Charles H. Gabriel

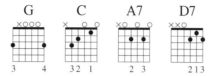

Verse 1

|**G** |
I was standing by my window

|**C** |**G**
On one cold and cloudy day,

|**G** |
When I saw the hearse come rollin'

|**A7** |**D7**
For to take my mother a - way.

Chorus

‖**G** |
Will the circle be un - broken

|**C** |**G**
By and by Lord, by and by?

|**C** |**G**
There's a better home a - waiting

|**D7** |**G** |
In the sky, in the sky.

Verse 2

    ‖**G** |
Oh, I told the under - taker,

    |**C** |**G**
"Under - taker, please drive slow,

    |**G** |
For this body you are hauling,

    |**A7** |**D7**
Lord, I hate to see her go."

Repeat Chorus

Verse 3

    ‖**G** |
I will follow close be - hind her,

    |**C** |**G**
Try to hold up and be brave,

    |**G** |
But I could not hide my sorrow

    |**A7** |**D7** ‖
When they laid her in the grave.

Repeat Chorus

The **Hottest** Tab Songbooks Available For Guitar & Bass

FROM

cherry lane
music company

PLAY IT LIKE IT IS **GUITAR** WITH TABLATURE — NOTE-FOR-NOTE TRANSCRIPTIONS

PLAY IT LIKE IT IS **BASS** WITH TABLATURE — NOTE-FOR-NOTE TRANSCRIPTIONS

Guitar Transcriptions

02501410	The Black Keys – Attack & Release	$19.99
02501629	The Black Keys – Brothers	$24.99
02501500	The Black Keys – A Collection	$22.99
02501766	The Black Keys – El Camino	$19.99
02501600	Black Label Society – Order of the Black	$22.99
02501510	Joe Bonamassa Collection	$24.99
00110278	Joe Bonamassa – Driving Towards the Daylight	$24.99
02501720	Joe Bonamassa – Dust Bowl	$29.99
00110294	Zac Brown Band – Uncaged	$22.99
02501565	Coheed and Cambria – Year of the Black Rainbow	$22.99
02506878	John Denver Anthology for Easy Guitar Revised Edition	$19.99
02506901	John Denver Authentic Guitar Style	$17.99
02506928	John Denver – Greatest Hits for Fingerstyle Guitar	$19.99
02500632	John Denver Collection Strum & Sing Series	$17.99
02501448	Best of Ronnie James Dio	$24.99
02500198	Best of Foreigner	$24.99
02501242	Guns N' Roses – Anthology	$29.99
02506953	Guns N' Roses – Appetite for Destruction	$24.99
02501286	Guns N' Roses Complete, Volume 1	$29.99
02501287	Guns N' Roses Complete, Volume 2	$29.99
02501755	Guns N' Roses – Greatest Hits	$29.99
02501193	Guns N' Roses – Use Your Illusion I	$27.99
02501194	Guns N' Roses – Use Your Illusion II	$24.99
02500458	Best of Warren Haynes	$29.99
02500476	Warren Haynes – Guide to Slide Guitar	$19.99
02501723	Warren Haynes – Man in Motion	$22.99
02500387	Best of Heart	$24.99
02500831	Jack Johnson – In Between Dreams	$22.99
02500653	Jack Johnson – On and On	$24.99
02500858	Jack Johnson – Strum & Sing	$19.99
02501564	Jack Johnson – To the Sea	$19.99

02500380	Lenny Kravitz – Greatest Hits	$22.99
02501093	Amos Lee	$19.95
02500129	Adrian Legg – Pickin' 'n' Squintin'	$19.95
02500362	Best of Little Feat	$22.99
02500305	Best of The Marshall Tucker Band	$24.99
02501077	Dave Matthews Band – Anthology	$22.99
02501502	John Mayer – Battle Studies	$22.99
02500986	John Mayer – Continuum	$24.99
02500705	John Mayer – Heavier Things	$24.99
02501513	John Mayer Live	$24.99
02500529	John Mayer – Room for Squares	$24.99
02506965	Metallica – ...And Justice for All	$24.99
02501626	Metallica – Classic Songs	$19.99
02501267	Metallica – Death Magnetic	$24.99
02506235	Metallica – 5 of the Best/Vol. 2	$12.95
02507018	Metallica – Kill 'Em All	$22.99
02501275	Metallica – Load	$29.99
02507920	Metallica – Master of Puppets	$24.99
02501195	Metallica – Metallica	$24.99
02501297	Metallica – ReLoad	$29.99
02507019	Metallica – Ride the Lightning	$24.99
02500279	Metallica – S&M Highlights	$27.99
02500846	Best of Steve Morse Band and Dixie Dregs	$19.95
02501324	Jason Mraz – We Sing, We Dance, We Steal Things.	$22.99
02500448	Best of Ted Nugent	$24.99
02500348	Ozzy Osbourne – Blizzard of Ozz	$22.99
02501277	Ozzy Osbourne – Diary of a Madman	$22.99
02507904	Ozzy Osbourne/Randy Rhoads Tribute	$24.99
02500680	Don't Stop Believin': The Steve Perry Anthology	$24.99
02500025	Primus Anthology – A–N (Guitar/Bass)	$22.99
02500091	Primus Anthology – O–Z (Guitar/Bass)	$27.99
02500468	Primus – Sailing the Seas of Cheese	$24.99
02500875	Queens of the Stone Age – Lullabies to Paralyze	$24.99
02501617	Joe Satriani – Black Swans and Wormhole Wizards	$24.99
02501299	Joe Satriani – Crystal Planet	$27.99

02501701	The Joe Satriani Collection	$24.99
02501205	Joe Satriani – The Extremist	$24.99
02500544	Joe Satriani – Strange Beautiful Music	$24.99
02500920	Joe Satriani – Super Colossal	$22.95
02506959	Joe Satriani – Surfing with the Alien	$22.99
02500188	Best of the Brian Setzer Orchestra	$22.99
02500985	Sex Pistols – Never Mind the Bollocks, Here's the Sex Pistols	$22.99
02500956	The Strokes – Is This It	$22.99
02501586	The Sword – Age of Winters	$19.99
02500799	Tenacious D	$22.99
02501035	Tenacious D – The Pick of Destiny	$19.99
02501263	Tesla – Time's Making Changes	$22.99
02501147	30 Easy Spanish Guitar Solos	$16.99
02500561	Learn Funk Guitar with Tower of Power's Jeff Tamelier	$22.99
02501440	Derek Trucks – Already Free	$24.99
02501007	Keith Urban – Love, Pain & The Whole Crazy Thing	$24.95
00102592	Jack White – Blunderbuss	$19.99
02500636	The White Stripes – Elephant	$24.99
02500583	The White Stripes – White Blood Cells	$22.99
02501092	Wilco – Sky Blue Sky	$24.99
02500431	Best of Johnny Winter	$24.99
02501716	Zakk Wylde Anthology	$24.99
02500700	Zakk Wylde – Legendary Licks	$19.95

Bass Transcriptions

02501108	Bass Virtuosos	$19.95
02500117	Black Sabbath – Riff by Riff Bass	$22.99
02506966	Guns N' Roses – Appetite for Destruction	$22.99
02501522	John Mayer Anthology for Bass, Vol. 1	$24.99
02500771	Best of Rancid for Bass	$24.99
02501120	Best of Tower of Power for Bass	$19.95
02500317	Victor Wooten Songbook	$24.99

See your local music dealer or contact:

cherry lane
music company

EXCLUSIVELY DISTRIBUTED BY

HAL•LEONARD®
7777 W. BLUEMOUND RD. P.O. BOX 13819 MILWAUKEE, WI 53213

halleonard.com